Copyright © 2023 Samuel John

The police are in charge of law enforcement and maintaining order.

Police officers are duty-bound to serve and protect citizens.

You can ask them for help if you are lost or if you find yourself in trouble.

They are also duty to prevent and avoid crime, such as robberies.

The police are also in charge of controlling traffic, so that there are no accidents and that safety regulations are respected.

CAFE
SWEET SHOP
SHOES

POLICE
451
PROTECT AND SERVE
SHOP

In the event of an urban accident, the police visits the scene to investigate what happened and assist those affected.

CAFE
THANK YOU
POLICE

Police officers patrol the city day and night to check that everything is in order.

At the police station, police officers conduct their research, process documents, receive complaints, and serve citizens.

There are cells inside the police station. They are used to lock up criminals until it is decided what to do with them: whether to release them or take them to jail.

Always remember that you must obey
and respect the police officers.

POLICE
OFFICER
ESSENTIAL ITEMS

POLICE

We use handcuffs or shackles to immobilize criminals.
EXIT

Radio allows us to quickly respond
to an emergency.
PIZZA

The badge is used to be identified as a police officer.
POLICE

The whistle is often used to get someone's attention.  Normally, organizing traffic.

The police baton is a necessary tool to defend themselves against possible attacks.

In extreme cases, the police officer may be forced to use his firearm when he sees his life or that of other people in danger.
451
PROTECT AND SERVE

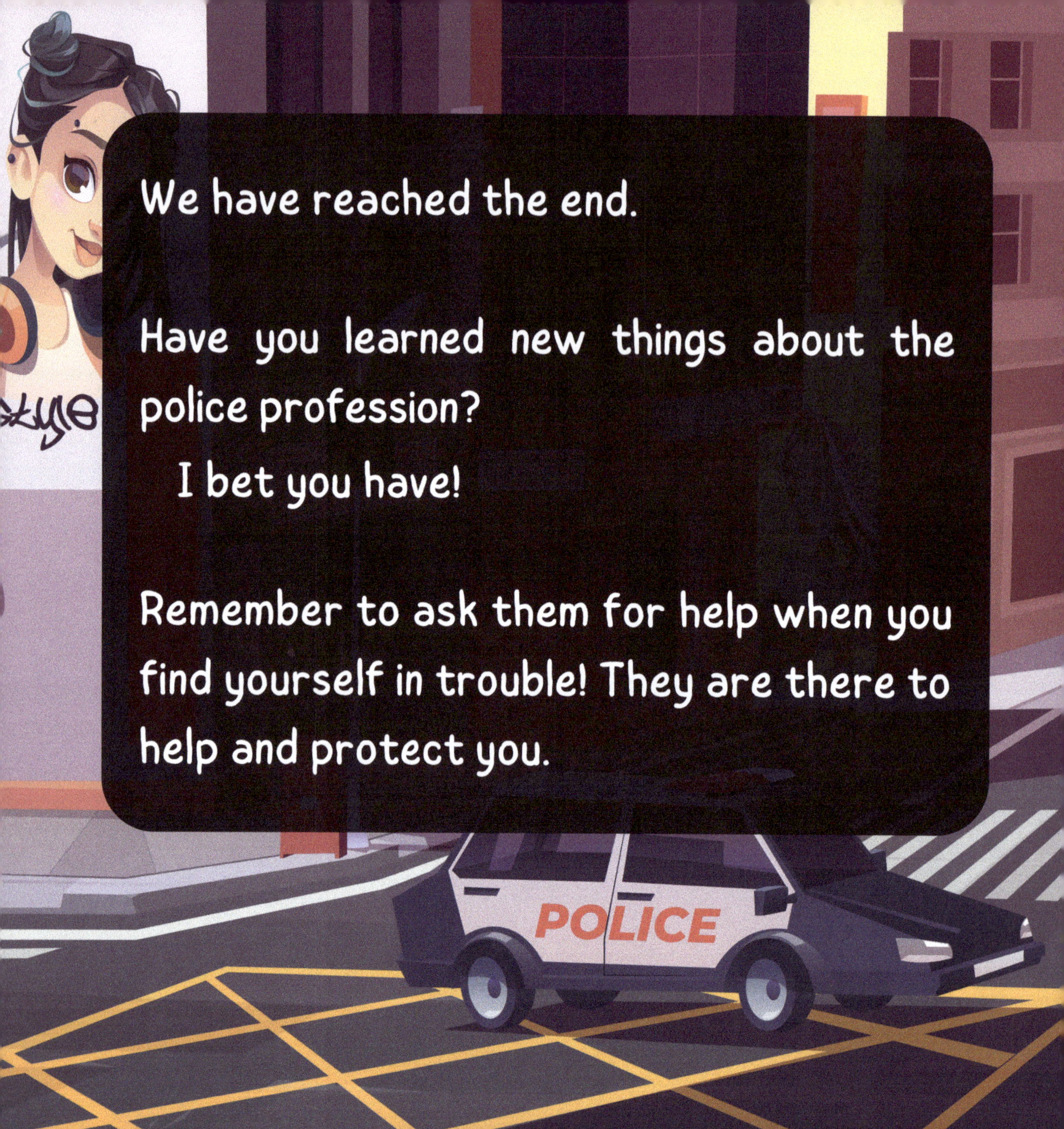

We have reached the end.

Have you learned new things about the police profession?
I bet you have!

Remember to ask them for help when you find yourself in trouble! They are there to help and protect you.

POLICE

I hope you liked it and that you learned new things.

I want to ask you a favor so that this book reaches more people, and that is that you rate it with a sincere opinion on the platform where you purchased it.

With that small gesture, you will be helping me to carry on with new projects.

I can't wait to start creating
my next book for you!

See you soon!

# KEEP LEARNING...

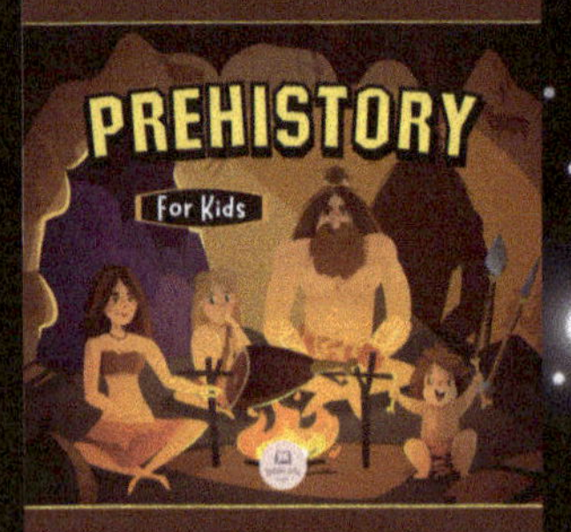


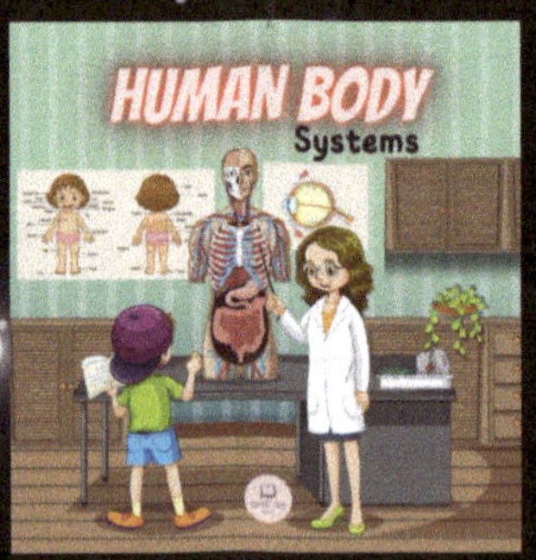

https://www.pge.me/childrensbooks